GET THERE!

❧❧

Najiyyah Mahdi

Fulton Books, Inc.
Meadville, PA

Published by Fulton Books 2020

ISBN 978-1-64654-256-7 (paperback)
ISBN 978-1-64654-257-4 (digital)

Printed in the United States of America

❀❀

CONTENTS

INTRODUCTION

In honor and praise to the God of all. This book was written from a place of love and a desire to assist myself and others in Returning to God. I included myself because I, too, am in the process of Returning to God. I realized there is no set time or any road map to get back to God.

This book started as a desire to write, which led to me wanting to share my experience with God's mercy and grace. It wasn't clear what I should write about and what was needed to start writing. So when I received an invitation via email to attend a free writing webinar, more specifically Hay House's "How to Become a Successful Author Live Masterclass," I was not surprised. I knew the power of stating desires and believing they will unfold. There are also no such things as coincidences or accidents... Things happen as they should.

The webinar made me realize the importance of knowing my intention in what I felt was needed for myself and others. The webinar consisted of four sessions. At the conclusion of each session, I asked the Holy Spirit (voice of God within me), Am I a writer? Do you have anything for me to write about? Finally, after the third session, I asked the Holy Spirit, Am I capable of writing, and what do I need to write about? Then the answer came. I have to tell my story in order to support others in their journey.

You will notice I used religious references (Holy Bible and the Holy Quran) throughout this book not to make a point about religion or to lead you down any religious path but only to provide you familiar references. I am not a religious scholar, so your interpretation of these scriptures may be different than mine, and I expect that. I also used them to emphasize that most doctrines indicate that we are more than what our minds can comprehend.

It might be difficult for you to understand who you are especially if you have never been told or shown who you are. I recommend you start with asking yourself who you are. If you hear the voice within you say anything other than you are a son or daughter of God and were made in the image of God, do not believe it.

I pray this book blesses you with peace, joy, and love.

ENTRANCE

Then God said, "Let us make mankind in our image, in our likeness, so they may rule over the fish in the sea and the birds in the sky, over the livestock and all the wild animals, and over all the creatures that move along the ground."

So God created mankind in his own image, in the image of God he created them; male and female he created them.

God blessed them and said to them, "Be fruitful and increase in number; fill the earth and subdue it. Rule over the fish in the sea and the birds in the sky and over every living creature that moves on the ground." (Genesis 1:26–28)

Recall when your Lord said to the angels: "I will indeed bring into being a human being out of dry ringing clay wrought from black mud.

When I have completed shaping him and have breathed into him of My Spirit, then fall you down before him in prostration." (Surah 15 Al Hijr [The Rock] Ayats 28–29)

Our existence began with God, not with our parents. Our parents are stewards. They are responsible for getting us here (the birthing process) and taking care of us until we can reestablish our relationship with God. Somehow many of us have gotten distracted by life and all its experiences and opportunities and forgot our true origin.

In the *Lion King*, there's a scene where Rafiki shows Simba his reflection in the water to remind him his father still lives with in him.

Rafiki: He lives in you.
Mufasa: Simba, have you forgotten me?
Simba: No! How could I?
Mufasa: You have forgotten who you are, and so, have forgotten me. Look inside yourself, Simba. You are more than what you have become... Remember who you are... You are my son and the one true king.

At some point in time in our lives, we are all Simba. The conversation that occurs in this scene is no different than the one our spiritual Father has with us. The spiritual Father I am referring to is the one who gave us his essence, purpose, reason for being. Throughout our lives, we will be given an opportunity to remember who we are and where we came from. Are you willing to take the opportunity?

My desire is for you to see yourself, your sisters, and brothers (all mankind) as you were created to be. You are holy, created in the image and likeness of God. You have been given power over all things. Do not allow your current circumstances which may include challenges or concerns with your health—physical, financial, emotional, or mental state—make you think you are someone other than who you are.

Avoid allowing anyone or anything to cause you to see yourself other than the way your holy Father sees you. You are divine, a ruler, and you have dominion over the creatures of the earth.

Your greatest life is still possible.

ROAD TRAVELED

The Lord himself goes before you and will be with you; he will never leave you or forsake you. Do not be afraid; do not be discouraged. (Deuteronomy 31:8)

My sheep hear my voice, and I know them, and they follow me: And I give unto them eternal life; and they shall never perish, neither shall any man pluck them out of my hand. (John: 10:27–28)

"You are the LORD, you alone. You have made heaven, the heaven of heavens, with all their host, the earth and all that is on it, the seas and all that is in them; and you preserve all of them; and the host of heaven worships you." (Nehemiah 9:6)

And when my servants ask you, [O Muhammad], concerning Me— indeed I am near. I respond to the invocation of the supplicant when he calls upon Me. So let them respond to Me [by obedience] and believe in Me that they may be [rightly] guided. (Surah 2 Al Baqarah (The Heifer) Ayat 186)

You are not offtrack and you have not run amok. You are right where you are supposed to be. Trust and allow yourself to return to the Creator from right where you are. I know God is right where you are. I am sure you are wondering, How is it possible that God is right there with you in your journey especially since some of you have been struggling with addictions to drugs, alcohol, food, etc. all your life? You have been incarcerated physically, mentally, and emotionally for what seems like a lifetime. You have done things folks would describe as horrific and unthinkable or other things you would rather not recall. Not knowing your self-worth may have also hindered you, I too struggled in that area. I understand what you are saying, but I am here to tell you, you are still on the path to return to God. You have taken the path that was and is yours to take.

Do not feel bad or have any shame in anything you have spoken, action you have taken, or thoughts you have had. Shame, guilt, regret, or any other negative emotion will keep you from seeing the light of day or the truth about yourself. In order to reestablish a relationship with God, you *must* see yourself loved, a child of God, a gift from God, prosperous, powerful. Stop seeing yourself through your eyes and realize you are priceless in the eyes of God.

It does not matter what you think is stopping you from returning. I am here to tell you, you can Return. Many speak of the afterlife or spiritual realm or once we have perished as the life we should seek. I am here as a living and breathing example that you can have it while you are here in this physical body. You can have peace, joy, love, and abundance here and now. I recommend you start with asking the Holy Spirit (living God or voice of God within you) the following questions: 1) Where do I start? 2) What do I need to do to return you? You can ask these questions out loud or ask within. I recommend finding a quiet, still place where you can be alone with God to ask these questions. Trust me, the answer will be the same whether you ask out loud or within. The answer will be the same. Afterward, make sure you create a quiet mental and physical space so you can hear the answer. You can quiet the mind by focusing on your breathing. A physical space can be a closet or any place that will allow you to physically disconnect from others.

To those of you who have loved ones (family, friends, etc.) you are worried about and don't know if they will make it back to God, *relax*. One way or another they will return, whether it's physical or spiritual. We all must return to where we came from. This may not sit well with you, but you need the truth, and we have to stop burdening and sickening ourselves because our loved ones are not willing to return to God when and how we think they should. All we can do is focus on our journey and be willing to give and show up at one hundred percent in our own journey.

The God of all things, the One who created you and me, the sun, moon, stars, sky, all the earth. The God of all. Just for a second, think about all that you know that exists, and see where it began. For example, you were born from your parents, and your grandparents had your parents and so on. Where did this birthing process begin? Here's one more example just in case that example didn't work. The shoes on your feet were a vision or thought in someone's mind before they were manufactured and worn on your feet. This example may not be significant as the creation of human life, but none the less it shows the power of creation as expressed by God. In other words, it started as a thought and became real.

You are not the worst thing you have ever done or said; you are the greatest thing God ever created.

DISTRACTIONS

Do not be conformed to this world, but be transformed by the renewal of your mind, that by testing you may discern what is the will of God, what is good and acceptable and perfect. (Romans 12:2)

Be careful for nothing; but in every thing by prayer and supplication with thanksgiving let your requests be made known unto God. And the peace of God, which passeth all understanding, shall keep your hearts and minds through Christ Jesus. Finally, brethren, whatsoever things are true, whatsoever things are honest, whatsoever things are just, whatsoever things are pure, whatsoever things are lovely, whatsoever things are of good report; if there be any virtue, and if there be any praise, think on these things. (Philippians 4:6–8)

Distractions are anything or anyone that gets you off course from returning to God. They are the thoughts of worthlessness, confusion, sadness, jealousy, or taking on someone else's emotional baggage, just to name a few. These are the things that when they show up, they steal your peace, joy, and love. I have never experienced a distraction that I liked. Distractions steal time and energy. After I encounter a distraction, I need a mental and emotional break to figure out where I was in the process of returning to God. As for me, distractions occur when I am on the edge of learning or realizing something critical about myself or my relationship with God.

I experienced a distraction recently, during my daily morning meditation. For some reason, I wasn't able to quiet my mind. I was focusing on my past, present, and future. I also found myself dwelling on other people's problems, challenges, and struggles. As a result, I decided to use the rest of the day to meditate. So I focused on God throughout the day by not allowing myself to focus on anything other than God. I accomplished this by focusing on my breathing and paying attention to my thoughts. In the beginning, it was difficult, but I eventually found my flow, and it was *amazing*. I was totally at peace—no thoughts, just silence. Suddenly I started to hear my coworkers' conversations. They started with office gossip, discussing who was getting promoted and why they should or shouldn't get promoted.

Before long, my quiet mind was a jungle gym. I started comparing myself with my coworkers and agreeing with the negative comments I was hearing about my coworkers. In other words, my mind attached to what I was hearing, and I was distracted. Eventually, I was able to take some deep breaths and return to a peaceful and quiet mind. The lessons in this moment was that every breath I take is a reminder that God gave me life, and only God can take it. Stop thinking others can give you peace or that they have the power to take your life… They can only distract you from the life God has for you. It doesn't matter what anyone tells you or you tell yourself. God is the giver, sustainer, and maintainer of life and will not forsake you or write you off.

Distractions will get you off course, and God will lead you back on track.

MY JOURNEY

The Spirit of God has made me;
the breath of the Almighty gives
me life. (Job 33:4)

I know God's present in my life. I know because it
was during some of my most difficult moments that
I felt God's presence. And every time I take a breath,
I know God's with me.

Part of my return to God began with religion.
For many years, I studied Islam and I thought it
was the only way for me to connect or worship the
Creator. One day, I found myself confused, and I felt
something missing in my life. I realized I was seeing
and believing in the God external to me. It took years
for me to realize God was within me. I had struggles
about whether or not God was real in my life, so I
started seeking clarity outside of Islam. Please don't
misunderstand my view on Islam. Islam has been

my saving grace. My faith and belief were founded through Islam. Islam was the truth for my life for many years until I realized I had to go deeper within.

I started asking myself questions such as, Where is God? Why do I believe Islam is the only way to get to God? Have I put God in a box? Are the religious and spiritual leaders of the past and present the only ones who are close and in alignment with God? Is God still alive? How do my prayers get answered? Can God hear my prayers, cries, worship, fears, beliefs and desires?

Some of these questions may be familiar to you, or you may have your own questions. All my questions have been answered by God. The only answers I'm unsure about are the ones I was too distracted to hear, see, or experience… That's my issue, not God's. Ask whatever questions you need to ask, believing the answers are there. This scripture should clear up any doubt you may have on whether your questions are answered or not. James 1:5–6, "If any of you lacks wisdom, you should ask God, who gives generously to all without finding fault, and it will be given to you. But when you ask, you must believe and not doubt, because the one who doubts is like a wave of the sea, blown and tossed by the wind." My questions came from a longing to know God on a more intimate level. There were also sadness, a broken heart, a missing piece, and not knowing who I was.

In my personal experience and having discussed religion with others, I've learned that religion is a vehicle or means to get to God, not a direct route. For instance, I have friends who are Jehovah's Witnesses, Christians, and Catholics, and they shared with me that when they stopped seeking religion and sought after God for themselves through prayer (conversation with God) and meditation, they felt more connected to God. They experienced God on a more intimate and personal level.

Dear friends of mine continue to express to me on a recurring basis, "I was made in the image of God, daughter of God, I have greatness inside of me, etc." I am starting to realize this to be true because every book, video, pastor, etc. I read or listen to confirms it. It has also been made clear in my prayers and meditation. However, it really resonated with me when my friend Janetta told me that no matter how much awareness I think I have, I have yet to tap into my greatness. If you get nothing else from this book, remember this: Surround yourself with friends that see you as more than you see yourself—friends and family that see you through the eyes of God.

In my mind and experience, I was a believer and all God's great work was external to me. And I was a believer believing God was external to me. I should be humble and grateful for whatever I have and where I am at (not desiring more). I am powerless and just here in this gigantic world, trying to survive in it. I thought I had to be this way because it pleased God only to find out that God wants me to thrive and to bless me abundantly. I didn't know my power and strength. I am a mind of God; all things were possible. The Holy Spirit lived in me. I was created in God's image and likeness. This is not for me to brag about but to show God is God and there's no limit or boundaries to what God can do or envision for our lives. God can do the unthinkable, the unimaginable. The more I meditate on this, the more peace, joy, love, and abundance I have in my life.

Remember earlier, I mentioned having a broken heart and being my authentic self. I recall one night when I was heartbroken because the best relationship I've ever been in came to a sudden end. We dated on and off for what seemed like a lifetime. Well, I guess twenty years is a lifetime. However, this time our "end" felt real. It seemed my partner experienced that I was not one hundred percent in the relationship. In comparison, this time, I had to do some soul-searching in order to deal with the pain. I started reliving my childhood—the "should-have-could-have moments" and choices I made in my life. Does this sound familiar, or am I the only one after a breakup that plays the relationship over and over in my mind to figure out what I did wrong. There was a point in the sadness that I could no longer breathe, so I prayed for God's presence and touch. Immediately, I felt this tight hug around my body, and I stopped crying. Did I forget to mention, I was the only one in the room…I believe that was God's love that embraced me.

In all honesty, during my dating years, I felt like a hypocrite. Why a hypocrite, you ask? I was dating a woman, and I believed I could not practice and believe in Islam and date a woman. So I had to go deep within to understand what I was struggling with and ask if it was really a struggle. I thought I couldn't be passionate about my faith and believe in God and be with a woman. How could I read the Quran and pray five times a day and be with a woman? You see where I am going. I thought loving someone created by God was wrong. This made me realize that love flows and goes deeper than a woman or a man. Love is God, so the relationship I was in wasn't about what I thought love was or my religious beliefs. It was based on my limited thinking and the box I had placed God in. It was through sadness, healing, and returning to God that I realized love is freedom, love is a gift, and love is God.

I don't know if, in my physical lifetime, I will ever fully and completely return to God. I am going to continue moving forward because the glimpses and the moments I have experienced have been amazing. The peace, love, and joy I feel when I am worshipping and conversing with God are priceless. Nothing else matters to me when I get to that place of peace no matter what I am going through.

Do not think we have to experience pain, sorrow, or sadness in order to Return. I am just sharing my journey. Get there however you Get There.

DESTINATION/ESTIMATED TIME OF ARRIVAL (ETA)

You were taught, with regard to your former way of life, to put off your old self, which is being corrupted by its deceitful desires; to be made new in the attitude of your minds; and to put on the new self, created to be like God in true righteousness and holiness. (Ephesians 4:22–24)

Do not be anxious about anything, but in every situation, by prayer and petition, with thanksgiving, present your requests to God. And the peace of God, which transcends all understanding, will guard your hearts and your minds in Christ Jesus.

Finally, brothers and sisters, whatever is true, whatever is noble, whatever is right, whatever is pure, whatever is lovely, whatever is admirable—if anything is excellent or praiseworthy—think about such things. (Philippians 4:6–8)

Delight yourself in the LORD, and he will give you the desires of your heart. (Psalm 37:4)

There is no ETA. I hate to disappoint you, but we all have to Get There in our own timing. However, I would caution you that the longer you take, the less time you'll have to experience peace, joy, love, and bliss in this physical realm called life. There needs to be a willingness and desire to change in order to Get There. Don't get scared and don't think it's impossible. Remember, God is with you.

First, start by asking God in belief and faith to change your thoughts, actions, desires, and words you speak. Next, or simultaneously, visualize yourself differently (picture yourself changed or doing something other than what you normally do). Afterward, through self-awareness, you should see the change in yourself, which will lead to you paying attention to your actions and ultimately leading to a desire to want to change more and more. You don't have to believe this process, but I am telling you what has worked for me and others. The saying goes, "See what you want to become or have." Try it. You can only grow from here. The examples I use are about things I physically obtained. The sole purpose of these stories is not to brag on me, but to brag on who God is in my life. My desire is to continue asking for the desires of my heart, believing it will happen, and receiving what God has for me.

I was desiring for a new job, and I was suffering and struggling, trying to make it happen in my own time. One day, I finally surrendered and asked God to give me peace, and I surrendered my desire. Surrendering and trusting God meant I had to stop wondering if, when, and where I would get a new job. A few weeks later, I was sitting in a meeting and I had a vision of a palm tree. You better believe I took notice. At the time, I had been working and living in northern Virginia for seven years, and I was burned-out from shoveling snow. Two months later, I was offered a job in Orlando, Florida, and I've lived here for three years.

The next example is about a gift from my beautiful wife, Keisha. Didn't I mention we got married? Surprise! I wanted to see if you were following along in the book. She wanted to buy me a new vehicle, an SUV type. At first, I wasn't on board because I didn't want us to increase our debt especially since our old vehicles were paid off. If anyone knew my wife, they'd know she's persistent. I finally gave in, but I was struggling to decide on what vehicle I wanted.

One day, during an "extensive conversation" (married couples know what I mean), and after conducting market research for two weeks, I still didn't know what I wanted. I asked her if we could end the conversation so I could be clear about my desire. This was on Thursday, and on Saturday, she got a call that the exact vehicle I wanted—which did not exist within the state of Florida or surrounding states—was four hours away and that the dealership was delivering it to Orlando. Keep in mind, I never told her… I took the desire to God. I've been driving Max, my SUV, ever since.

The goal is to return to God. In returning, we are guaranteed peace, joy, love, bliss, etc. Bliss is possible in the spiritual realm and in the physical life.

This can be accomplished through daily prayer and meditation; interactions of kindness, compassion, and love with others. So relax and don't worry about getting to your destination quickly. However, there needs to be a willingness and a desire to Get There. Your willingness will definitely impact how soon you arrive. Although this is our birthright and our reason for existence, we have the freedom to choose. The prayer below is an offering from me to you. In addition, I shared with you a powerful expression from Ms. Maya Angelou.

> Lord, I return to You.
> You are my salvation, and in You, I have my being.
> I give you my thoughts, actions, and desires.
> I trust You with my gifts and talents, known and unknown, to manifest Your vision.

In the words of Maya Angelou, "When I found that I knew not only that there was a God but that I was a child of God, when I understood that, when I comprehended that, more than that, when I internalized that, ingested that, I became courageous."

CONCLUSION

We all have our own journey. We have to travel to return to the Creator. So I recommend you take the pressure of yourself and stop comparing your journey to anyone else's. No matter what you encounter in your journey, remember, the Creator is in you and with you in your journey. Trust where you are at every moment. No matter how pleasant or uncomfortable it may seem, it is designed for you to Get There.

Align with the Divine in you...trust your Higher Self to return you to the Creator.

GLOSSARY

Ayat—verse in the Quran

God—Lord, Source Energy, Father, Creator of All

Holy Spirit—voice of God within God's creations, Living God

Image—Physical likeness of someone or something made to be seen

Life—emotional, physical, and spiritual existence in the human body.

Likeness—Resemblance

Surah—chapter in the Quran

DEDICATION

"To my beautiful, loving, gifted and talented wife thank you for supporting me even when it seems I'm dancing to a different drum beat.

To my resilient, powerful, and creative family and friends may you always know you are sons and daughters of God. Remember, you are one moment away from seeing the desires of your heart come to pass.

My prayer is that we all continue to believe there are no limits to our greatness and all things are possible."

ABOUT THE AUTHOR

Najiyyah Mahdi is a new author that will astound you with her willingness to be transparent and to honor her truth in order to support others in honoring their truth. She is creative, mentally and emotionally empowering and a spiritually inspired certified life coach. As a life coach, her passion and desire are to inspire, serve, and support others during all of life's rewarding and challenging moments.

Born and raised as Andrea Nicole "Nikki" Norman in East Orange, New Jersey, to Andrew and Eula Norman (both deceased), she's an eleven-year Army veteran, who continues to serve her country as a US Army acquisition professional.